Teachers Speak

What I ALWAYS wanted to tell my *PRINCIPAL* but NEVER *DARED*

JULIE BACHER, M. ED

Dedication

This book is dedicated to...

My father, Don Bacher for always supporting me and making me laugh.

The teachers who never get recognized for what they do.

My former coworkers for your friendship and laughter. You made a tough job, fun.

My former students. I hope you

a) had fun
b) learned something (Hopefully? Maybe? Humor me here people....)

As a leader, it's a major responsibility on your shoulders to practice the behavior you want others to follow.

—Himanshu Bhatia
Founder and CEO
Rose International Inc.

Unless someone like you cares a whole awful lot, nothing is going to get better. It's not.

— The Lorax (Dr. Seuss)

Julie Bacher as The Cat in the Hat for "Everybody Reads" week.
Photo credit: Patty Thomas

Table of Contents

Teachers Speak:
What I always wanted to tell my principal but never dared

What does a principal do?

What is a principal's purpose? Paperwork? Discipline? After relocating to California from Vermont, I realized that there were things left unsaid about the experience of being a teacher, and the critical role administrators play. One of the roles of a principal is to give teachers feedback on their performance, but principals don't receive feedback from the teachers. I am not convinced that principals understand the importance and influence of their behavior on teachers and students. A principal can make or break the cultural climate of the school. And although they mean well, and are overworked (like teachers), it's important that we finally break this silence. We live in a culture of denial. Teachers are under so much pressure from students, parents, the administration, and the community. It's often impossible, or unsafe, to admit when they need help; they risk being deemed incompetent. I asked teachers from around the United States about their experiences and opinions.

There is something wrong in schools. There is something wrong in the culture of teaching. Here is a list of "typical" remarks I've heard from teachers over the years. They vary from altruistic to overwhelmed. There is blaming, and there is bragging. This is the **public face** of teachers:

"There are not enough hours in the day; we should make the school day longer so we can teach more."

"It's not fair we have to deal with emotionally disturbed kids. If parents would actually 'parent' their kids, the kids would not disrupt our school day."

"He always behaves for ME! He knows that I MEAN BUSINESS."

"Just one more thing, just one more thing. They keep piling more and more on our plate. It's always just one more thing."

"It's all about the kids. Everything is always all about the kids."

"If there were REAL consequences, then the behavior would actually stop. Instead, they go to the principal's office and their 'consequence' is they get to play with the turtle!"

"I care so much about these poor kids; it just breaks my heart. I want to take all of them home with me."

This book, conversely, will deliver messages that you might never hear a teacher say, but things that we actually think and need. This is the **private face** of teachers.

We all have an idea of what a teacher is and what a teacher does and says. My intent in writing this book was to explore what teachers really experience, think, and feel. What do they need from administrators, and what are administrators already doing that improves their experience? Mostly, I wanted to make clear that administrators are pivotal to the teaching experience. Are they on your side? Are they against you? Is it safe to be honest and open with them? Do they know what's really going on in the school?

I asked twenty teachers ten specific questions. I put out a Facebook query requesting volunteers to be interviewed. Of my personal friends, a couple people responded. When I put the query on a Facebook group called #teacherproblems, the response was overwhelming. Everyone wanted to participate, and enthusiastically so. There were GIFs of people jumping up and down saying, "Me, me, me!" It was playful and positive. From my first post, of my personal friends, people wondered whether they even qualified to be interviewed. One was "only" a retired teacher, not currently teaching. Another was taking a few years off and wondered if she counted because she wasn't "under contract" as a teacher. Some asked if I would mind having a "special education," or "SLP (speech and language pathologist)" perspective, as if these professionals would not be counted as "teachers." School culture is a world where people are stacked against each other in terms of who is perceived to be valuable and important, and who is not.

Many teachers were confused by my purpose. I didn't want to hear the things that teachers always say. We've all heard that a hundred times before. I wanted people to be real. What did they really need from administrators? What had been good? What had been bad? What had been terrible? What had been wonderful? Basically, if anyone had a story, I wanted to hear from them.

Here are the questions I asked:

1. Describe your journey to becoming a teacher.
2. What do you love about teaching?
3. What do you hate?
4. What is your best moment as a teacher?
5. What was your worst moment?
6. Tell me about a time when your principal really came through for you.
7. Tell me about a time when your principal really let you down.
8. What would you like to tell your principal (if there were absolutely no consequences)?
9. What would you like to hear your principal finally say?
10. What else would you like to say?

I decided to write the interviews up in a third-person narrative, with the exception of "what would you like to say to your principal," and "what would you like to hear them say." I wanted those answers to really ring true, to be the teacher's authentic voice. In true teacher fashion, not everyone answered every single question—teachers don't follow directions well. (I'm allowed to say things like that because I've taught for 23 years). But they did share their story and their point of view. I'm eternally grateful for the participants of these interviews. Some of them are my close, personal friends, some were acquaintances, and some were complete strangers to me. In spite of this, everyone was honest and open, kind and genuine. We are all united in needing our story to be heard.

Here are the interviews:

Laurie

Age 58

Retired after 34 years
Spanish, English, and ESL

Laurie is a wise woman with a warm, inviting smile. She emanates love, knowledge, and compassion. Many people look up to her, and she is always there to help. Laurie really cares about people's feelings and experiences, especially those of her students.

Laurie had always wanted to be a teacher, ever since she was a kid. She actually had to fight to become a teacher, because people all around her were discouraging. "Don't be a teacher," they would say, or "You're too smart to be a teacher." They even asked her why she would ever want to be one. But she was determined and persisted against all those negative influences. Finally, she fulfilled her dream.

She loves how working with kids makes her a better person. She would not be the person she is or have the life she has if it were not for her kids. They are truly a gift. Laurie hates the overuse of compiled data. Yes, there are places to examine data, and it can sometimes be helpful, but it can also be a time sucker.

Laurie was very lucky early in her career to have great administrators. They almost all had her back. She taught the kids that no one else wanted to teach, and anything that Laurie wanted to do with the kids, they gave her the "go ahead." Her administrators enabled her to be a much better teacher, and she probably would not have made it without their help.

There were many times in her career, however, when Laurie felt let down by her principals. One time in particular, she was teaching a Spanish 4 class. These kids were not the "college-track" kids. They had gotten all the way to Spanish 4 because of Laurie, because of her connecting with them and not giving up on them. During one of her observations in this class, Laurie told the principal that a particular student would be an interpreter for her, because the whole class would be in Spanish. The principal replied that she didn't need one, because that's not what she was going to be looking for. Laurie assured her that it would really be helpful, but the principal still refused.

The lesson Laurie chose for that day was an evocative one. It was about immigration. She started by asking the kids questions to see what it would take to make them leave their country. Would they be able to stay if they had to move into a smaller home? What if they had to share a bedroom? What if they had to share a bed with someone in their family? What if they could only eat the food from the little store, and it wasn't enough? The students replied that these questions weren't realistic; that would never happen. Laurie explained that it does, and that's why immigrants migrate to other countries; the living conditions in their home country become unbearable for them. This was one of Laurie's most powerful lessons, and she was proud of it.

When she touched base with the principal about how the lesson had gone, her response was quite unexpected. "You've got a bunch of knuckleheads in there! When I saw the kids you were teaching, I didn't even pay attention. I was answering some emails." Laurie was dismayed and shocked. The principal had missed the point.

Laurie's best moments are when the class will run itself, whether she is in the room or not. They can run the class because of the structure and the expectations she has set, and they can keep it in Spanish. She also loves it when parents tell her that their child won't stop speaking Spanish at home.

Her worst moments are when they lose a student—when a student dies. It's so painful for everyone involved. It's completely overwhelming. Kids can't help but think, "When I die, will I have been important to anyone? Will anyone even care, or notice?"

What would you like to tell your principal (if there were no consequences)?

My goal in the classroom is to help my students listen in order to understand. If that were the main goal of administration, it would be a game-changer. If the administration were focused on really listening to understand, it would change everything. Everything would fall into place.

What would you like to hear your principal finally say?

I understand your situation and challenges. I'll do anything in my power to support you.

I don't know if I would have survived if I hadn't had that support when I first started teaching.

Maria

Age 45

Maria is a slender woman who appears younger than her forty-five years. She is comfortable in her skin and always quick with a joke. She has a fashionable, hippie sense of style. Her energy is friendly, light, and open. However, there is a sense that she is not entirely unburdened.

Maria's journey to becoming a teacher began in college. She was good with kids, having been a babysitter, and felt that she had a natural ability to teach. In high school she had been assigned a project to interview 5 people who had jobs she might want to have when she was older. Maria had interviewed an elementary teacher and it seemed like a good fit for her. Becoming a teacher seemed to be a logical progression of her life.

Even though she had studied to be a teacher, Maria did not immediately go into teaching after graduation, though she did work with kids. She worked at an after-school program for a while. However, she was looking for a more meaningful career, one in which she could really help people. She had her degree, and she liked the idea of a school schedule.

Maria loves tapping into kids' creativity and really following their lead. When she would put on plays in her classroom, everyone got excited about it. They were all engaged, and everyone had their own part. Whether it was practicing their lines or making props or a backdrop, everyone was enjoying it. That's what she loves, when kids take the lead and really see their creativity shine through.

She hates the system, the prescribed "what to teach." A lot of it is not developmentally appropriate. It goes against everything the child needs, and yet it must be done. When kids get to kindergarten, all they want to do is play. Yet, they are supposed to start the day with Superkids, and then do a half hour of "Bridges" every single day. The standards keep becoming more stringent. It is now expected that kids will be reading by the end of kindergarten, while it used to be by the end of first grade. It is just not appropriate for that age.

Maria's best moment is when kids take the lead. They are really in the flow of learning and using their creativity. It's usually with some sort of themed group project, such as putting on a play, and all the kids look forward to it.

Her worst moment is feeling like she is forcing kids to go against their needs and to do things they really don't want to do. Children want to play and be imaginative. The things we require of them don't support their needs and instincts.

A time when her principal had her back was when Maria started teaching a mindfulness program in her classroom. Mindfulness is a practice similar to meditation, when people reflect on their physical and emotional experiences, without judging them. The goal of Maria's curriculum was to help kids be happy and successful, and there have been many studies proving the effectiveness of mindfulness. A parent got angry about the lessons and called the school. She thought it was some sort of hippie meditation, and her Christian family was wary of such activities. Even though the principal herself was wary of mindfulness, she defended Maria and her program. Maria wasn't there to hear the phone call, but she knew that her principal had supported her.

A time when Maria was let down by her principal was when the school had started an outdoor education program in the lower grades. There has been ample research that indicates having kids play and explore in the forest is extremely beneficial for their learning and growth. The outdoor education program consisted mainly of taking the kids into the woods behind the school and just letting them use their senses and explore. The whole team had been really gung-ho and cohesive about it. The principal supported it at first, though she didn't entirely understand the philosophy behind it. As time went on, the principal, Kathy, became more and more anxious. Eventually she didn't support it at all, and the program was halted until Kathy retired. They were able to restart it again with a new principal.

What would you like to tell your principal (if there were no consequences)?

Just relax. Let teachers do what they do and trust that they are the experts. The micromanaging gets worse and worse every year. But we are okay; just trust us. You don't need to be in charge of so much. Enjoy this more. Relax.

What would you like to hear your principal finally say?

I'd like to hear some acknowledgement of my specific strengths in the classroom. I'd like for her to know what I was doing in class, and how I was doing it. She was not in touch with that.

What else would you like to say?

It's getting more and more difficult every year to be a teacher. There are more and more mandates, and it just gets harder. Teachers need to be trusted. They need more support and kudos all around, from the administration and from the community. We need to do what's best for kids AND teachers. There is some of that happening now, with trauma-informed practices, but kids need more mindfulness, arts, hands-on activities. Teachers need more time to collaborate. We need to intentionally build community at school and in the community at large.

Maria left teaching two years ago due to stress. She doesn't miss teaching.

Emma

Age 26

3 years
English, Gen Ed.

Emma is a thoughtful young woman with green eyes. Her fashion sense is practical and unfettered. She is quick with a smile or a joke and has an uncanny ability to imitate her students to a T when relating stories. Her speech is clear and honest when speaking about kids and their behaviors, or about anything at all.

Emma was always comfortable in school, like she was in her element. She had two teachers who influenced her to become a teacher. One was a very good example; one was a very bad example. The good teacher taught English. Emma always felt engaged in the lesson and she enjoyed it. All the students were engaged in learning. The bad teacher taught math. She was not great. She would explain something once, put the homework assignment on the board, and leave the students to do it. She was a teacher but didn't really teach. Emma was scarred for life when it came to math. Emma thought, "I could do better."

Emma loves the moment when kids get this look on their face like "Oh my gosh!" It happens sometimes when there is a plot twist in the book they are reading, or with any sudden understanding. Emma never gets tired of seeing that look.

There is nothing Emma hates about teaching, but there are a few things she dislikes. Sometimes, even though she does get a planning period, she always feels rushed. She also doesn't like that she has to take work home every night.

Her best teaching moment was a lesson for her high school English students before they read the book The Lord of the Flies. Emma put them in small groups and told them to collect 6 fire, 6 shelter, 6 water, and 6 food tokens. There were only 2 rules: a) try to collect all the tokens they needed, and b) stop when she said stop. Each group received an envelope containing 4 tokens of each necessity. Emma just sat back and watched. At first, the groups tried to trade with other groups. However, they soon realized that no one had enough in the first place. Soon the groups started to steal from each other, tricking each other into not watching their stash, and hiding them as soon as they could. Before long the kids were yelling, and they were all over the place. It was pure anarchy. Then Emma said, "Stop."

When the kids in the book started turning against each other, her students said that if THEY had been there, none of the conflict would have happened. Emma reminded her students of the pre-reading activity they had done, and how smoothly that had gone (not smoothly at all). Suddenly the lesson hit home for her students—because they had lived it.

Emma's most challenging moment occurred during her first year of teaching. She had a "directed studies" class consisting of seventh and eighth grade together. She saw this group at the beginning and end of the day. They were terribly behaved, saying they didn't have any work when they actually did, fooling around, and just being general nuisances, as only middle-schoolers can be. It was unpleasant and stressful, but she survived it. Everything now seems easy compared to that year.

Her principal, Jane, really came through for Emma by hiring her in the first place. Emma was right out of college and had not taught before. It was a huge risk, and Emma could not be more grateful. Jane has "had her back" whenever a parent has been unhappy with Emma, either for sending their kid out of class, or because they didn't approve of the book the class was reading. Jane always defended her in parent conferences. She has never let Emma down.

What would you like to tell your principal (if there were no consequences)?

I'd just like to say thank you for having my back.

What would you like to hear your principal finally say?

I'm pretty sure she's said this before, but I'd like to hear: "She's doing a good job."

Robyn

Age 55

27 years
Spanish

Robyn has short brown hair with a warm face. She is direct, relatable, and friendly. There is something about her energy that makes me comfortable; she's not pretentious.

Robyn fell into teaching when she got divorced and realized she needed more money. Her original plan was to get married and have children. That worked for a while, but an unexpected divorce meant she needed to rely on herself financially. Unlike many teachers who go through special training and classes to become a teacher, Robyn did it backward. She had majored in Spanish, and a local school had an urgent need for a teacher. They agreed to hire her if she would get certified. Robyn loved the kids but didn't know what she was doing as far as teaching. In 2002 she attended the NTPRS conference and learned about CI (Comprehensible Input) and TPRS (Teaching Proficiency Through Reading and Storytelling). TPRS language acquisition method is considered best practice based on the latest research on how the brain learns. Through this conference, Robyn learned to be confident in the classroom.

Robyn really loves when a student connects to something. She hates all the grading.

The principal at Robyn's first school was great. He understood that she had not gone through a teacher training program, so he was always available to support her, even just to offer encouragement or a joke in the hallway. She never felt micromanaged. On one occasion, Robyn accidentally said the word "ass" in the classroom. She immediately went to the principal and told him what she had said. His response was, "Well, you are human."

That year was a hard one for the school's budget. Many teachers ended up getting RIFed (reduction in force aka laid off), including Robyn. When her principal told her in his office, he teared up, saying he wished he didn't have to do this. He gave her a wonderful letter of recommendation. He also thanked her for her work and wished her the best. Even though Robyn was worried about getting a paycheck, she wasn't angry. She appreciated the kindness with which she was let go.

Her best teaching moment was in a Spanish 1 class. Robyn wasn't sure what to do, so she decided they would make up a "class story" on the overhead projector. This story ended up being silly and ridiculous, and all the kids were really into it. The protagonist of the story was Billy Idol, who was quite popular at the time. At the end of the class a student said, "Billy Idol en la medianoche dice más y más y más." These were the lyrics to a popular song (Rebel Yell), and the student had spontaneously translated them into Spanish. Robyn felt proud and relieved that the class had been so much fun that day. It was a positive, memorable experience.

One of Robyn's worst moments occurred while she was teaching an eighth-grade class. There was some time left and she decided to do some TPR to fill the time. She would say (or point to) a word, and the students would gesture or act it out to show understanding. Some of the 8th grade boys started exaggerating the gestures and making them vulgar, of a sexual nature. Robyn didn't even know how to go about punishing them. Not knowing what to do, she didn't tell anyone; but she felt awful.

In April of last year Robyn stopped teaching for medical reasons. She was having a hard time building relationships with kids like she used to do. She still has students who send her things on Facebook that remind them of her, or something she might like. But, these relationships did not come easy due to her medical situation. She was really struggling, and no one even checked on her to see if she was okay or to ask how she was doing. At her first job, her principal made it a point to ask her how things were going, but no one at her last school showed any concern when she truly needed it.

Robyn struggled for a few reasons. She was new to the school and had switched schools a few times. She was battling depression, which she had been dealing with at a low level for a while, but suddenly it was starting to negatively affect her job and her well-being.

After she went on leave, she returned on the day after school ended to collect the rest of her belongings. Her two administrators saw her but didn't even greet her or ask how she was doing. Robyn collected her things and left.

What would you like to hear your principal finally say?

Well, they say a lot of nice things. In my experience they talk the talk, but there is no follow-through. For me it's more about saying something and meaning it; it's about honesty. I had a principal who had an email signature that said something about not judging because you never know how much someone is struggling. This same person never lent me a helping hand when I was struggling, as her email would have me believe.

Also, when they do the evaluations, why can't they talk normally? They feel the need to use "edu-babble." Why can't they admit at the start of the evaluation meeting how unfair the meetings are?

Administrators should get to know teachers on a personal level and make more of an effort to do so at the beginning of the year. They should be interested in us, our strengths, and what we would like to work on this year.

Sarah

Age 37

Sarah has an expressive face with warm blue eyes, and straight blond hair. She exudes humor and friendship, honesty and openness.

Both of Sarah's parents were teachers, as were many other relatives. Some think it's in the blood to be a teacher. At the beginning of high school, Sarah wanted to be a medical student. As she realized how much schooling it would take to become a doctor, she decided against that plan. Instead she turned toward music and teaching.

Sarah's students love her. Her sense of humor makes them enjoy band and music lessons. She is serious, yet playful. Middle schoolers appreciate her wit. In her first year as a music teacher, Sarah had received a state award for her teaching. After that year she changed schools. She considers getting that award to be her best moment as a teacher. When she took the band outside to practice marching for the parade, all the other kids would look out the windows with envy. It looked like so much fun because they were outside. Sarah was always smiling and shouting directions, making light of the experience, yet at the same time teaching them to march correctly.

Sarah loves making a difference in kids' lives, whether they know it or not. She loves being able to give them a life-lesson along with their music lesson.

Sarah hates grading. She hates the principal and the superintendent at her second school for what they put her through; a lack of support and undermining Sarah when she needed help. They were running the school and the district but didn't have teaching experience themselves. They had no idea what it was like to be in the classroom.

Sarah did like the principal at her previous school. He had been a teacher the year before he became principal, so he respected Sarah as a true colleague. In fact, he had been her eighth-grade math teacher! If he had a question about something Sarah was doing, he would ask her. There was no assuming, and she never felt threatened. He was always friendly and trusting.

The principal at her new school, Daisy, had no idea what Sarah was doing in the classroom, even while she was observing. Daisy didn't understand Sarah's discipline system; she didn't understand music, the music curriculum, or any of the content Sarah was teaching. Sarah describes a lot of "bullshit" going on; it was as if Daisy was on a mission to make her miserable. Sarah has asked for help with her band class. There were 40 students in there and Sarah was having trouble controlling them all. When she asked for support, Daisy didn't help her. Sarah went to the union about this, but they didn't help her much.

At that same time, the fifth and sixth grade teachers started arguing that band was NOT necessary and that it was detracting from the students' time in other subjects. Sarah's argument was that even if music weren't important, and even if they weren't learning anything (which of course they were), can't the students have some fun during their day? Can't they have something to look forward to? What's wrong with enjoying a class during the school day?

The administration at this school let Sarah down every day for six years. The worst was when they called a special board meeting to move the band program to after school, so it wouldn't interfere with the students' academic day. The board approved the move, and Sarah lost 25% of her band students. She also had to teach after school, rather than during school.

Sarah was very depressed during this time. Coming into work was a chore she dreaded. However, she didn't want to face the consequences of NOT coming to work. More than that though, she didn't want to let her students down. She knew they counted on her. During this dark time, Sarah posted something on Facebook about how hard it was to just go into work and how unhappy she was. Somehow—she has no idea how—it got back to the elementary principal, Mr. Jones. (This school had two principals, Mr. Jones for elementary and Daisy for middle school.)

After hearing about her alarming Facebook post, Mr. Jones went to Sarah's room to check on her. Sarah was sitting in the dark. He walked up to her and asked her how she was doing. She just lost it and started crying. Sarah told him about a letter Daisy had given her that morning that terrified her. It said

Sarah was scheduled for a meeting, and she should bring a union representative. She told him about how Daisy seemed to just want to make her life miserable, and how it was getting harder and harder for her to come into work every day. Mr. Jones was a great listener. He took some time with Sarah to really do some problem-solving. He said he would go to the central office to explore her options and would get back to her later that day.

When Mr. Jones returned that afternoon, he had found an option for Sarah. She was able to take some medical leave, while she tried to relax and figure things out. At first it was only going to be for two weeks, but she ended up extending it to two months. Because it was medical leave, she did get paid during this time.

At the end of the two months, it was clear to Sarah that she did not want to go back to work. She wrote a letter of resignation. Sarah's old friend from high school was working in the central office at the time, and she knew that. That's why she sealed the envelope, so he wouldn't be able to read it. Sarah drove to the central office and handed in her letter. As she walked out that door, she felt as if the weight of the world had been lifted off her shoulders. She almost felt as if she could fly. It was such a relief for Sarah to never have to go back to that place where she had been treated so badly and had had so much stress.

Sarah was unemployed for most of the next year. She was still happy with her decision to leave the school. It was the right thing for her. She found work substitute teaching in five schools around the area, when it was available. She worked for a few temp agencies and landed a job with a law firm answering phones and working at the front desk. She loved that job! People there were really friendly; they liked Sarah a lot too.

Now Sarah works at a group home for clients with mental health and substance use issues. However, she still has some PTSD from the school job. One day her boss said he needed to see her upstairs in a few minutes. Sarah's mind started spiraling downward...worrying about all the terrible things he might be about to tell her. Was she fired, or had she made a mistake, or was she in trouble? When Sarah got upstairs, she told her boss how she was feeling, and about the letter she had received at her previous school. She explained how much fear that had instilled in her. Her boss was very understanding. He had just wanted to tell her she was doing a good job and update her on some client issues. To this day it has become something they can joke about: "Sarah, I need to see you upstairs. Bwahaha."

At her new job, Sarah has never felt threatened. Even though she did not go to school for social work, and has certainly made her share of mistakes, her bosses talk about it with her and troubleshoot for next time. She feels that she is finally in the right place for her.

**What would you like to tell your principal
(if there were no consequences)?**

What I want to say, you wouldn't be able to write in your book. I want to say, "Fuck you. I'm worth more than you ever thought."

What would you like to hear your principal finally say?

I trust you. I've got your back. I support you.

What else would you like to say?

I only hate three people in this world. Daisy (my principal) is one. The superintendent is the second, and one of the parents who made my life miserable is the third.

I left teaching because of the administration. Not because of the students. Not because of the parents.

Michele

Age 56

7 years
Grade 2

Michele has short, curly brown hair and a ruddy complexion. Her face shows she has been through a lot, and her experience comes through as wisdom and kindness.

Michele wanted to be a teacher since the age of fifteen. Her father wanted her to be a nurse, not a teacher. She proceeded to flunk out of college, then go on to become a housewife and raise her three children. She became a teacher at the age of forty-eight.

One thing Michele hates about teaching is the growing number of mandates; the things teachers are required to do that just keep multiplying. She loves to see kids make a connection to something; when they finally "get" it, it gives her goosebumps.

Her lowest moment was on a field trip at her former school. She was responsible for her class, and her principal asked her to take on more kids because the principal had to leave early. Michele refused because she felt it would be too many kids to supervise well and keep safe. Because of her refusal, the principal proceeded to demean Michele in front of the kids, teachers, and parents. Scolding her, she said that Michele sucked because she didn't follow her lead and that Michele needed to be "more supportive of her." Michele cried—in front of everyone on the field trip. She told the principal, "I will never put my kids below your needs!" Michele kept her kids safe and they stayed for the rest of the field trip. She ended up leaving that school because of the hostile principal who had humiliated her in front of the community.

The time when a principal really came through for her was when Michele was having family issues and needed to take time off. Her mother was dying of cancer, and Michele wanted to spend the last moments with her mom. After that, Michele's husband needed dialysis to keep him alive, and he was also put on the waiting list for a new kidney. At a moment's notice, Michele would have to take her husband to the hospital an hour and a half away to possibly get a kidney that had just been harvested.

Her principal told her, "You are a great teacher. Family comes first. Period." Michele was able to take all the time she needed. It was amazing. Michele says of this principal: "She was amazing."

A difficult thing at Michele's school is that she feels let down in general communication. Things they are supposed to know are not communicated clearly. Traffic, where to park, allergies, testing, and late arrival notices for students are often not communicated until it's too late.

**What would you like to tell your principal
(if there were no consequences)?**

I don't want to lose her. I would not be able to work with someone who told me what to do and tried to control the details of my job. I don't have to have my plan book checked, for example, because that would be a disaster!

We are given certain leeway in our class schedule to attend to the students' social and emotional needs. From kindergarten to third grade, children need that social/emotional learning in order to prosper. Now we have the freedom and flexibility to give that to our students.

What else would you like to say?

We need to go back to having foreign language in the lower grades. It helps kids connect with other types of people, it expands their minds, and it helps them connect with kids who are different. Also, kids learn through play, and that has been taken away. We need to go back to having more play in the school day.

Laura

Age 36

11 years
Grade 5

Laura is young-looking and boldly confident. She was eager to share her story.

The high school Laura attended in rural Kentucky was not known for its academics. By senior year she had pretty much mastered everything they had to offer. There was a job fair that year where students went to shadow someone at their workplace, to see if they might like that job. Laura wanted to be a journalist, but she shadowed her mother's best friend who taught fourth and fifth grade. Laura decided she wanted to be a teacher because of all the fun activities they did during that day.

Laura majored in education in college. She worked for the Kentucky Mission Board, then at a Baptist center in Alabama. Through these two organizations she started working with underprivileged youth in the section 8 projects. There she realized this was this population that she wanted to serve.

Laura hates politics and being micromanaged. Laura's school district had a very difficult superintendent. He wanted to extend the school day by two hours and to extend the school year by 15 days. He said that anyone who didn't support his proposal was racist. They did end up extending the school day. It now runs from 7:45 am to 4:15pm. He originally proposed that the school day go to 4:45 pm. Thankfully, the board voted that down. That's the kind of politics she's talking about.

She loves that it's never the same day twice.

Her best moment as a teacher is when her former students come back to see her. They make time in the morning before school starts just to come and say hello. The elementary school starts an hour earlier than the middle school, so the older kids have time to spare in the morning. It touches her heart that they choose to visit her, their former fifth grade teacher.

Her worst moment as a teacher was when she needed to get a personal order of protection against a student's mother. This child, who had a lot of issues, said that Laura had hit her. Whenever there is an accusation made against a teacher in her district, that teacher is put on administrative leave while an investigation takes place. The principal came into Laura's room in the middle of a lesson (It was April so they were preparing for state testing.) and told her she needed to get her things and leave the building immediately; there had been an accusation made against her. It wasn't really scary for Laura, just sad. She was starting some important units with her students, not to mention getting ready for the testing. But she had to stay out of school for 20 days, as the investigation was conducted.

The school's security cameras showed that Laura never hit the student. In fact, the student had hit her while they were in a secluded part of the hallway. The child's mother, who had said that the school had been lying about the whole thing, became belligerent and threatening after Laura's innocence was proven. This led to the order of protection; that mother then needed a police escort if she wanted to enter the school building. Though she was vindicated, it was still so sad for Laura to miss that critical time with her students.

Laura has worked in four different schools. Her current principal is supportive. He has a great sense of humor, but often has knee-jerk reactions. He goes too far sometimes or doesn't know where to draw the line. Laura was on a new team with two new teachers. They were not familiar with the curriculum or the school, so in team meetings Laura ended up doing most of the talking. The other two, lacking experience, just didn't know what to say. One day the principal pulled Laura aside and told her she needed to talk less during the meetings. She was told to talk only 10 % of the time, and the other two were each to talk 45% of the time. This seemed ludicrous to Laura. She liked and respected the principal, but the mandate to limit her speech in the meetings was going too far.

Laura has had two terrible principals and two great ones. The great ones supported her as the teacher and took her side when conflicts arose or in intense discipline situations. They had her back, but the other two did not.

One female principal told Laura she shouldn't wear pants to school because it wasn't professional: she should only wear skirts and dresses. She was also judgmental of Laura's personal life, telling her she shouldn't date people of other races.

What would you like to tell your principal (if there were no consequences)?

I am an intelligent, valued professional who can make decisions that are best for kids. I have three degrees, and they don't give you three degrees if you're an idiot. You should acknowledge the enormous workload we have and listen to and value teachers' decisions and opinions.

What would you like to hear your principal finally say?

I need you.

A few years ago, one of the schools I was in had an enormous turnover. Ninety-five percent of the staff left, including me. I'd like to hear him say: "I need you. I want you to stay. I need you here."

Mary

Age 49

15 years
Elementary Music

Mary is slender and tall, with long blonde hair. Her energy is whimsical, artsy, and thoughtful.

Mary never intended to become a teacher. People were always telling her she would make a good music teacher. The school acquired a waiver, allowing her to work there while she worked on getting her license. Mary then got her license through peer review. Mary likes teaching, but she doesn't love it. If it were not for summer vacation, she would probably not be a teacher.

I asked her if her friends were right, that she would make a good music teacher. She answered yes, basically, except she is not good at certain aspects of teaching, such as planning and record keeping. Classroom management is difficult for her, but it is for everyone to some extent.

Mary loves that she gets to do music for most of the day. She loves seeing the joy and accomplishment children feel when they can finally make music.

She hates the micromanagement; the stuff you have to do that doesn't actually help you become a better teacher. She also hates the fact that teachers don't have a choice about this. It's frustrating, and it feels like her time is being wasted.

Her best moment as a teacher is hearing people say, "This is the best concert our school ever had!" She also enjoys seeing her former students start a band in high school on the instruments she taught them how to play.

One of her lowest moments happened last year. It was her first year teaching elementary music at a new school. One sixth grade girl, who had had difficulty all year, was refusing to participate. Mary had offered her the choice (like she was supposed to do) of either participating or sitting in the back of the room quietly, at least not disrupting the rest of the class. The girl sat in the back of the room and became louder and more disruptive, just making noises. Suddenly she threw a chair. Another student stormed to the back of the room and immediately set the chair straight up and told her not to do that; it wasn't ok. Mary watched the entire thing, feeling more scared the whole time, thinking the two students might actually fight each other, not knowing what was going to happen. The entire class had to leave the classroom and go somewhere else because of the girl's threatening behavior.

This incident made Mary want to quit. It also upset her that this student was in such distress. What was it that had set her off? She hated the thought that it was something about her, Mary, that caused this incident to happen.

The principal was amazing. She really acknowledged how Mary was feeling and was very supportive. She had someone cover Mary's next class, in case she needed to take more time to stop crying. This was more support than Mary had even expected. The principal even gave Mary a hug and assured her that this was not her fault. Afterward, there was a meeting about the incident, and everything was worked out.

A time when she felt the principal let her down was at the concerts. It's part of Mary's job to put on concerts for the community, and the principal didn't even show up. Mary had imagined that the principal might introduce her, then she would come out, say a few words, and begin the concert. Instead, Mary realized that the principal wasn't even there. It was disappointing on a few different levels. Wouldn't the principal want to see it, to see the kids shine and enjoy music? Wouldn't it be part of Mary's evaluation as a music teacher?

All the kids generally do great at the concerts. They enjoy performing for their parents. Of all the things about teaching, concerts are where Mary and the kids really shine. Afterward they receive many compliments. It seems so odd and invalidating that the principal wouldn't be there to hear the music and the compliments. Apparently, the principal didn't think they were important.

Mary also doesn't feel supported by the curriculum coordinator. There are many meetings and professional development days that have nothing to do with Mary's music curriculum, yet she is required to participate in them. When she brings it to the attention of the curriculum coordinator, he says that he realizes that, but she has to do it anyway. It seems like a big waste of time; focusing only on math and literacy devalues her subject matter, again treating music as if it isn't important.

**What would you like to tell your principal
(if there were no consequences)?**

I've been very lucky with the principals that I've had. I belong to Facebook groups of teachers and I've heard horror stories. I want them to know that the principal makes an enormous difference in the school.

What would you like to hear your principal finally say?

For once, I'd like to hear them publicly acknowledge that we are all of equal importance to the school.

Cassi

Age 37

Cassi is friendly and focused. She has shoulder-length dark blond hair and glasses that are just as stylish as they are useful. Her persona on Facebook is light and humorous, yet in person she is laser-focused on the questions at hand.

Cassi had wanted to be a teacher for as long as she could remember. In high school, Cassi developed a severe anxiety disorder. The school created an IEP with accommodations for her. She didn't have time limits during test-taking, for example, and she was allowed to take tests in a separate room from the rest of her class. These accommodations really saved her, and it cemented the idea that she wanted to become a teacher. She realized that special education was for all sorts of students. There were many kinds of learning disorders, such as hers. Her perception of special education before her IEP was that it was only for students who had Down syndrome. But Cassi felt validated by and extremely appreciative of her accommodations.

She loves making connections with her students. She loves watching them grow personally and academically and form their own personalities. The hardest thing is that she has four aides in her classroom right now. They are all older than Cassi, and she is in charge of them. Sometimes it's hard to tell someone who's older than you what to do or that something needs to be done differently. On the same note, it's hard for them to take direction from Cassi, as they have been part of the school for much longer than she has.

One of her best moments occurred when she was working with a third-grade girl who had autism. Cassi taught her to say the sounds of the letters B and A, and then put them together to start reading a word. Her whole face lit up with pride! Another highlight was when the class was making Valentine 's Day cards. This same little girl was told by the occupational therapist that she could only make one. Was she going to make it for her father, or her teacher? The little girl, Lizzy, chose to make one for Cassi.

Her principal has always had her back. If Cassi ever has any questions, she answers them and takes care of things. She is always there if Cassi needs anything at all and will defend and support Cassi in parent meetings. Cassi appreciates that her principal is always calm. She is easy to talk to about anything.

Cassi has never really been let down by her principal. She is worried that she may lose her job because of budget cuts and wishes her principal could stop that from happening. However, Cassi knows the principal has no control over this.

What would you like to tell your principal (if there were no consequences)?

I would like for her to come into my room and observe more often. Well, I'd like her to, but at the same time I don't want her to, because it makes me nervous. But more feedback would probably be a good thing.

What would you like to hear your principal finally say?

I see kids engaged in class, and all the lessons are differentiated. Good job.

What else would you like to say?

I'd just like to say I appreciate all that she does for me, and all her kindness on a personal level. It means a lot.

Kamille

Age 32

Kamille is a bubbly and warm woman. She has an easy smile and a truthful, yet tough, demeanor. You can tell that she has been through a lot and has a huge heart.

When I asked Kamille to tell me about her journey to become a teacher, she laughed and said, "What a journey it was!" Initially, Kamille wanted to be an OBGYN. She studied premed, but in her sophomore year, something happened that she had never experienced before. She failed a test in her Chemistry 2 class. Being a perfectionist, this was devastating for Kamille to deal with. Why was this happening? Kamille realized that she needed to change her major, so she decided to study psychology. During her internship, she was placed in an elementary school. The school counselor was supposed to supervise her but was never around. Instead, Kamille was placed in a fifth-grade classroom to ensure that each student's IEP (individual education plan) was being followed. She fell in love with it. The teacher became a mentor to Kamille, and she realized that school was the place she wanted to be. So, once again, she changed her major and studied for two and a half more years to get her teaching degree.

Kamille loves helping kids find what they love, things they'd never pursued before. She loves introducing kids to new experiences and watching their personalities develop. She loves watching kids find different parts of themselves. She hates that everything is so political. Kamille is the kind of person who wears her emotions on her face; she can't hide how she feels. She hates being given busywork to validate someone else's job. Also, administration doesn't see teachers as human. Teachers are told that they need to come in even if they are sick. They are not allowed to stay home.

One of Kamille's best moments occurred a few years ago. She had a very difficult class. One girl, Jackie, had especially bad behavior. She had a hard life at home, and really gave Kamille a run for her money. Everything was a battle with this girl. One day, toward the end of the year, Kamille entered her classroom to find that Jackie had written a letter on the board. It was a letter of appreciation to Kamille for all that she has done and for being such a nice teacher. Jackie had signed the letter at the bottom of the board. Not only that, but she made all the other students in the class sign the letter as well. To this day, Kamille feels a warm, fuzzy feeling when thinking about this. She had tried so hard with Jackie all year, and nothing seemed to be working. The letter on the board showed that even though it didn't seem like it sometimes, Kamille was really making a difference in this child's life.

Her absolute worst moment occurred at that same school, that same year. It was the only time that Kamille has ever been fired. She was a third-year teacher at that point, so she was still learning the ropes. There had been a lot of instability in the school that year. The principal had gone out on maternity leave, and the dean of students was completely incompetent. The class sizes were enormous, and students' behaviors were really challenging. There was no support. It was an inner-city school, and staff turnover made existent behavior problems even worse.

Being a charter school, test scores had to meet a certain standard. The administrators were pushing scores, so the kids had to test at a grade level ahead of where they were. Kamille's students didn't get the grades they were supposed to on the standardized tests. At the end of the year, her supervisor took her into the office for the end of year review. She asked Kamille how she thought the year had gone. Kamille, being the honest person that she is, poured her heart out. It had been one of the hardest years for her, and she got emotional. After that, her supervisor said, "We are not going to ask you back."

Kamille couldn't believe it. As a perfectionist, she puts her all into everything, and nothing like this had ever happened before. Not only that, but her supervisor had let her pour her heart out, just to fire her minutes later. She told her that she didn't know why she made her go through all that just to tell her she was not coming back. Why didn't she stop her sooner? Kamille now realizes that this decision had to do entirely with politics, and not so much with her as a person. Charter schools are really a dog-eat-dog world.

When I asked Kamille to recall a time when her administrator really came through for her, nothing came to her mind. There were many times she was let down, though. Once, at the school where the dean of students was incompetent, they were having a parent meeting. The dean was there, as were

Kamille, the parent, and a couple other teachers. The parent had complaints about the school, and this meeting was to address those issues. While the parent was talking, the dean of students stood up abruptly. He said, "I don't know why we are still talking about this. This meeting is over." He walked out the door. The parent had literally been in the middle of her sentence. Everyone in the meeting looked at each other as if to say, "What just happened here?"

Even without the dean of students there, they continued talking. There was no reason to cut the meeting short when they had been addressing some important issues. The dean then re-entered the office, telling everyone he didn't know why they were still having the meeting after he had declared it over.

What would you like to tell your principal (if there were no consequences)?

Status and appearance aren't everything. We are here for the students. You forget that we're here for the kids. It's time to stop only caring about money. Low performing schools and overcrowded classes are only profitable for the people at the top. You need to switch the focus back onto the kids.

What would you like to hear your principal finally say?

This is just busywork.

Faux motivation and things like that make no sense.

What else would you like to say?

Education is not led by educators; it's led by money. Low performing schools and overcrowded classes are only profitable for administrators. You need to switch the focus back onto the kids. Kids are kids, no matter what color they are, no matter what their socio-economic status is. It's time for administrators to value what really matters: the students that we serve.

Michael

Age 55

20 years
Upper elementary

Michael looks like a hippie with his long hair and beard. He is a skilled musician and tends to make things fun wherever he goes with his off-beat sense of humor.

Michael came into teaching later in life. He was a high school dropout and got a high school equivalency degree from a continuation school in California. His father was a teacher. Because of his sordid past, Michael didn't think he could ever be a teacher. He also didn't feel confident academically. However, he did want to make a difference in kids' lives.

It was his wife Kathy who encouraged him to become a teacher. She was a music teacher, and she believed in him. She encouraged him to go to community college to get his degree. At that point Michael had started recovery from alcoholism and drug addiction. Teaching has been a transformative experience for him personally as well as spiritually.

Michael loves having the same schedule as his wife. He loves seeing students' success. He loves seeing them become able to really have a meaningful conversation with someone and become productive community members.

Michael hates being the disciplinarian. He also hates being the judge and jury when it comes time for report cards and grades.

He describes one of his former principals as a "real ass-hat." She was a horrible principal and a horrible person. During the summer, Michael has a painting business. This person, "Ms. Smith," serves as a reverse role-model for the way he runs his business. When thinking about how to treat his employees, Michael asks himself, "What would Ms. Smith do?" Then he proceeds to do the opposite. That's how much (or how little) he respects her.

Michael's best moment as a teacher was when he was collaborating with another school to reenact the Battle of Hubbardton, the only battle of the civil war that was fought on Vermont soil. He really felt that the kids became a piece of living history. They reenacted the battle while forming a strong community with the other school. They really made history come to life. It didn't matter where the kids were from; they were all working toward the same purpose and achieving the same goal

One of his worst moments was when his previous principal threw him under the bus. The Friday before Memorial Day Weekend, she gave him a letter in a sealed envelope. She instructed him not to open it until he got home. It turned out to be a letter of reprimand that was going to be put in his file. A parent had been complaining about the school and about her child's performance. Instead of taking responsibility and dealing with these issues with the parent, the principal blamed everything on Michael. Everything the letter accused him of doing (or not doing) was a complete lie. She had fabricated this letter to make Michael look bad and to take the heat off herself. The parents had been requesting that she (the principal) step up to the situation. But all she did was blame Michael.

Michael went immediately to his union representative and grieved every accusation the letter had mentioned. One by one, he was exonerated of everything he was accused of in the letter, and nothing was added to his file. Receiving this letter was one of the most surprising and unfair things that has ever happened to him.

On another occasion, Michael was involved in a school play. They had been rehearsing it for two days straight, and it was finally the day of the performance, which was to be held that night at the town hall. During rehearsal, a boy tripped and hurt his back. Michael looked at it, and it looked a little bit bruised. It obviously hurt, but it didn't seem like a huge problem. He told the student to put an ice pack on it and he should be fine until it was time to go home.

After the performance that night, the boy's mother came up to Michael and lambasted him. She demanded to know why she hadn't been contacted when something so severe had happened to her son. What kind of a negligent teacher was he? This parent went up one side of him and down the other. Out of the corner of his eye, Michael saw his principal. She stood back and watched, listening, but not stepping in or saying a word. He felt completely abandoned at that moment.

His current principal has been great. She is constantly supportive of him. Last year, he had a very hard class. It was a combined class of fourth, fifth, and sixth graders. This class almost put him over the edge. There were twenty-three students, most of whom had IEPs (Individual Education Plans) and severe behavioral issues. Michael was teaching them language arts. They were unruly. They would flip him off (give him the middle finger) while he was teaching and throw blackberries, which are plentiful in the fall, at his back. His principal was always in there, supporting him. She would do anything to make his job easier, and she acknowledged the difficult behaviors he was dealing with. He is eternally grateful for this support.

What would you like to tell your principal (if there were no consequences)?

Administrators should realize that every teacher makes hundreds, sometimes thousands, of decisions every day. We are human. We always have the students' best interest at heart, but we will make mistakes from time to time.

Treat others the way you want to be treated. Don't be nasty to teachers.

What would you like to hear your principal finally say?

In a perfect world, as someone who is in recovery and living a life of self-reflection, I would like to see principals be reflective on their own actions and words. There should be a 12-step program to help narcissist principals to treat people more kindly.

Carla

Age 46

2 years
K-12 SPED, Middle School Behavior Specialist

Carla is a funky lady. Her pink glasses are large and decorative. She has short, straight blond hair, light blue eyes, and an easy smile. Her energy is bright and knowledgeable.

Carla got her teaching license in 2018 in K-12 special education. Before that, she had been a paraprofessional. Other teachers were always asking her why she didn't become a teacher. They loved the way she worked with the students and thought teaching would be perfect for her. She did a great job writing and following IEPs and supporting special education students with visual supports and hands-on activities. The only thing that kept her from becoming a teacher sooner is that she had a young child at home. She wanted to be there with him as much as possible, to really put her energy into him. She wanted to be a role model in that way.

Carla loves that teaching is like a puzzle. You are always customizing your delivery and approach to really reach students. She loves the communication element and finding a style that works for each child. She loves that she is on her own; she feels like no one is watching her. That level of control is really nice. She has control over what she presents and how. Carla loves data and data monitoring, especially when it comes to tracking behaviors with her heavy-hitter kids. She loves organizing the data. She loves seeing progress and talking to the families, making that connection with them to find what really works together. She also loves being part of a community of educators.

Carla didn't really like the word "hate" when I asked her what she hated about teaching. But she did understand what I was getting at. Carla recounts a situation that occurred in a previous school. It was difficult for her to be the behavior support person, because she felt really isolated. She had a hard time finding commonality with other teachers. She was also in charge of a group of IAs (instructional assistants), who often didn't follow through on what was asked of them. She hated having to supervise and manage other adults. Most of them had been there for years before she even got there, so taking direction from her was not always smooth, which she understood, but it really did make Carla's job more difficult.

The first year teaching special education, Carla brought work, and her computer, home every night. She could never "turn-off" work in her head. She was always thinking about her lessons, and her IEP goals for kids; she just couldn't disconnect from that emotional piece. She found that she wanted to talk about things with her family, just to really process what was going on, but she knew she shouldn't because of confidentiality. Even so, it was an ongoing inner battle to want to talk about school. She definitely had a great deal of emotional fatigue from school, even when she was at home.

Her best moment occurred while Carla was student-teaching. She was teaching high school English and had developed a good routine. The students would come in and immediately start their warm-up assignment in Google classroom, which would give her immediate feedback on how and what the kids were doing. She could project it onto the board and narrate how many had finished and how many they were still waiting for. It took the guesswork out of who was working and who wasn't, and it took the power struggle out of that situation. Not only that, but she could use the feedback she got from that warm-up activity to direct her lesson and to see what she needed to focus on for that day. Kids were very receptive to this routine. These warm-up activities helped the students with a writing piece they were working on about their post-secondary plans.

Her worst moment occurred this past school year. Since she works in the behavior room, Carla Deals with some intense situations. One day, two students were verbally aggressive toward her. They called her the N word bitch. One of the girls said it in the classroom; the other said it in the hallway. Carla is white, and these two girls are African-American. Since her job is to talk with kids about their behavior and to process it, Carla wanted to talk about it with them. She asked them why they had called her the N word bitch. She used the words they had said. Immediately, one of the girls started screaming that Carla had called HER those names, when Carla just was trying to process the behavior with them.

Carla had been these girls' advocate. Carla recognized that they were certainly outliers of the school society. She had stuck up for them and worked with their families. She had kept them from being suspended in the past by explaining that their behavior was a clear manifestation of their disability. She was on these girls' side when no one else had been. And now she was being accused of calling them a racial slur!

When the incident with these girls had happened, there was no one around to help Carla. The two IAs who were supposed to be there were nowhere in sight. The entire situation escalated quickly. There was yelling, and she tried to use the phone to call the office, but one of the girls slammed the door into her, which left Carla bruised. Carla was asked to leave the building, and not to return for two weeks. That turned into two months, because she was asked to not return until they had a meeting with the kids and their parents.

The incident had happened in December. In January, a meeting was held. The students were still angry and accusing her. They were not ready to talk to her at all. The parents attacked her verbally at the meeting. It was a disaster for Carla. The whole situation was so complicated. She was told to have NO CONTACT with the parents, kids, or anyone at the school. And all Carla wanted to do was to apologize and explain herself. She never even got a chance to explain her side of what had happened.

At the end of February, there was going to be a board meeting to terminate her. There had been no due process. She had had nothing but glowing evaluations. There had been none of the legal union proceedings. In fact, Carla was supposed to have been observed by her principal in December, but that had never even happened.

The situation had gotten so out of hand. Carla decided to resign instead of being fired. She didn't want to have that on her record. The union had actually been trying to help her get transferred to another school, but the pre-termination meeting was too close.

One time that a principal really had Carla's back when she was student teaching. The principal offered Carla a job inside the school so she could earn money while she got her degree. That principal arranged for Carla to have health insurance, benefits, and a paycheck. The philosophy was to "grow your own." There was a real community feeling in that school. Carla felt valued there.

She was let down during that incident with the students, which ended in a huge debacle, and eventually Carla's resignation. The principal should have had her back. Carla had specifically asked if she would have a mentor when she had interviewed for that job. She was told that she would, however she was not assigned a mentor. Instead there was an itinerant teacher who showed up once a week. She was allowed to ask him questions, but he had his hands full with other responsibilities and didn't have time or energy to mentor Carla.

What would you like to tell your principal (if there were no consequences)?

The opinions that other staff members have of me shouldn't be used against me. New teachers should have the support they need. It should NOT be a once-a-week check-in. It should be on a regular basis with feedback, and then more feedback. Also, they should start with the positive, just like we do in IEP meetings. This makes people feel good, and new teachers could use that. They should really monitor how the teacher is doing.

Also, I could have used some help managing my time. I knew when I had class and when I had planning, but there are things I wasn't able to get done because I kept getting interrupted. When am I supposed to do those things? Also, I want them to make sure I am taking my lunch. Half the time I couldn't take it because I was so busy catching up or helping students. I'm the behavior specialist, and behaviors happen all day long; they don't stop because it's my lunch time. There was no one backing me up.

What would you like to hear your principal finally say?

Let's recognize Carla for all the hard work she's done this week. She took care of seventy referrals! Let all acknowledge and thank Carla with a round of applause.

Thanking people should be on a cycle. I hear the same people being thanked over and over again. They should make sure everyone gets thanked, maybe even by receiving a postcard in the mail or something. I'd like for them to recognize that this job is hard and to acknowledge me in front of others. Come to think of it, I was never even publicly welcomed to the school.

What else would you like to say?

I hate how other teachers just send kids to me. They don't even call first. They are supposed to call and write out a pass. Kids show up to my room while I'm in the middle of teaching, and they don't even have a pass. Also, aren't classroom teachers supposed to be managing their own classes? Isn't that part of teaching too? They just send students to me without even trying to work it out first in the classroom.

I think that about covers it.

Today Carla is working on her master's thesis. It's a study of teacher speech and how it affects students' behavior and learning outcomes. She is excited about her research.

Ashley

Age 31

7 years
Grades 7-12 English

I was blown away by how much Ashley had to say. She is open and passionate about teaching and helping her students, many of whom have difficult life circumstances.

Ashley decided to become the teacher she needed as a kid. Her mom was great, but she worked all the time and was always tired. She was not the kind of mom who would get down on the floor and play with her kids. Her dad was a drug addict. Teachers were the most consistent relationship in her life. She always knew they loved her and cared about her.

Ashley doesn't know if it was the drug abuse or his mental illness, but her dad had a terrible temper. He would fly off the handle and hit them with a paddle or a belt for little things, and she didn't understand why. He played the guitar, so he would take one drug to stay up at night playing music, and then take another to come back down. Ashley didn't understand what her father was doing at the time, but she recognized that it was not normal. He moved out when she was in eighth grade, just about the time that she would have started to realize what was going on.

In grades 4-6 Ashley started playing volleyball and other sports after school. Her dad always failed to show up when it was time to go home, so Ashley would ask to use the school phone to call him. Usually he was passed out on the couch. One day there was a sign in the office: "Students may not use the phone to call home." She felt devastated. How was she going to get in touch with her dad? Looking back, she now realizes how unfair it was that the school wouldn't let her call home when she needed to.

Ashley's family lived in the country, but in one night there was both a tornado and a drive-by shooting. A stray bullet entered Ashley's house, and lodged in the chair where her mother was sitting. It got stuck in the chair but not before grazing her mom's leg, making a big, nasty bruise. When the police came to investigate, they examined the chair and shook it. When the family heard something rattling around in there, they were terrified that it was going to be her father's drug pipe or something. But the police found nothing more than a bullet.

At first, Ashley wanted to be an art teacher. One day in English class, she realized she was really enjoying it. Ashley loved how the teacher made class fun by discussing different ideas and literature. So, she decided to become an English teacher. Ashley loves kids, but (she knows this is going to sound bad) she's glad she doesn't have any at her house. It's cool that she gets to be a role model in their lives. She helps them get into colleges and trade schools. Ashley never had that encouragement, so she loves being part of that guiding light.

Ashley hates all the demands that the state and district put on teachers. Everything she does, every decision she makes, is for the kids. She hates being pulled in so many different directions. The school needs to just trust and support her as a teacher.

One of Ashley's best teaching moments occurred at her last school. There were two brothers whose dad had died years before, and their mother was a heavy drug user. Their mom was going to be tested for heroin the next day, and she knew she was going to test positive. In the middle of the night, she took the boys to California, telling them they were going on vacation. When they got there, she told them they weren't going back. Soon afterward the two boys did return, by themselves. They ended up living with the mother's brother's ex-girlfriend.

The brothers developed their own drug problem and landed in the hospital after an overdose. Eventually, they were able to return to school. Ashley had the pleasure of helping them and watching them graduate. They both have jobs now and one has a family. Ashley would like to think that she helped them get there. She feels proud when people say, "Bruno and Jake wouldn't have made it if it wasn't for you."

One of her worst moments as a teacher took place this past year. She had a female student who was very quiet. Her boyfriend was in the class as well. They would sit together, and he was always turning around and talking to her. Ashley told them they both needed to knock it off and stop talking. When they didn't listen, Ashley took the girl aside and told her she would move her into the hall if she had to. They still didn't stop, so she moved the boyfriend to the front of the class, and had the girl keep her seat in the back.

One day the principal came in to see Ashley and shut the door. The girl had called her mother, and her mother had called the principal. The girl said that Ashley hated her and accused Ashley of having feelings for the boyfriend. Ashley was shocked and literally gasped out loud. The principal said, "I can see from your reaction that it's not true."

Ashley was crushed to know that the student didn't trust her. She said that Ashley was always touching the boyfriend. Sometimes she does touch kids on the back, but never anything inappropriate. And Ashley wants you to understand that she's a big girl too, not the type that boys generally have crushes on. She was so frazzled she didn't know what to do, so she stopped talking to both of them. She had to put up a block between herself and them. Ashley doesn't ever want a kid not to trust her or not to feel welcome in her classroom.

Her one pet peeve is that there is no trust in teachers. One teacher does something wrong, then every teacher is a villain.

As for a time when an administrator really came through for her, Ashley doesn't have one.

There was, however, a time an administrator let her down. In her old school there was a lady who had been a para (para-professional; a classroom aid for one student), and suddenly she had an administrative position. She didn't even have a degree. This lady had a habit of throwing teachers under the bus, but she also had her favorites.

One day, Ashley had a student in her room who kept rolling his chair across the floor. (This was in a guided study hall.) She sent him out because he wasn't following her rules with the chair. A couple minutes later, this administrator sent the student back into the room. Ashley told her that he couldn't come back in because he wouldn't follow the rules. The administrator said that Ashley had to let him in because he had the right to an education too. Ashley felt like she'd lost control of her classroom.

What would you like to tell your principal (if there were no consequences)?

I think my biggest pet peeve is that administrators need to trust and support teachers. Stop giving us so many pointless directives and guidelines and just support and trust us. We know what to do. We are professionals.

What would you like to hear your principal finally say?

I'd like to hear them say that they trust me, and that I'm doing the right thing in my class. Teaching is a very thankless job. It would be nice to get some acknowledgement. Teachers work so hard for kids, and all parents want to do is blame us. It would be nice to hear that they appreciate what we do.

What else would you like to say?

Professional development as a whole needs to be reevaluated. So much of it is pointless. If you want good teachers, you need to give them good training. Help us find those tools that really help us grow as teachers. That way professional development has value to us.

Andra

Age 59

Andra has short, curly hair and a warm, friendly demeanor. She is stylish and quirky, always wearing mismatched earrings that somehow fit her outfit.

Andra became a preschool teacher because, in a nutshell, her mother was a preschool teacher, and she thought it would be easy. Andra worked with her mother after school when she was a kid, so she had already been around small children all her life. She breezed through all her college classes

Andra is enchanted by watching a child grow, learn to think, and figure things out. The best feeling in the world is when kids have a conflict then figure out how to use words to solve it. She feels proud that she has given them the ability to solve their own problems.

Andra hates it when people who don't know children tell her what to do. The administration doesn't understand childhood growth, and they are always giving her new rules and mandates that reflect that ignorance.

There have been so many "best" moments as a teacher; it's hard for Andra to choose just one. Here is one of her favorites: Andra's mother, Fran, is retired now and lives near enough to volunteer in her classroom. One day when her mother was volunteering, a child said to her, "Fran, I love you." Fran answered, "I love you too." The child continued, "You know why I love you? Because you made Andra, and I love Andra."

An administrator really came through for Andra at a time when she had been teaching preschool in the morning and running a private after-school program for preschoolers to make ends meet. Overall, she was getting paid much less than a full-time teacher. She hadn't worked full-time in years. (That's why, after teaching for thirty-four years, Andra isn't able to even think about retiring.)

Suddenly a lot more students were enrolling in the preschool. Andra was on a hiring committee that was formed to find another preschool teacher. They had interviewed a few people but were still in a quandary about filling the spot. The principal spoke up in one of the meetings and said, "I don't understand why we are looking elsewhere when we have an amazing preschool teacher sitting right here who would probably like a full-time job. Why in the world don't we offer it to her?" This was on August 15th, eleven days before school was going to start. Andra felt validated, and grateful. She also had to hurry and get ready for twice as many kids!

As for a time when a principal let her down, there have been numerous occasions in the past year, but one stands out. The school had a small group of preschoolers coming in on Mondays and another small group coming in on Wednesdays.

Each group had 2 and a half days of school per week. The principal asked Andra what she thought they should do with the program, and she said they should put the two groups together and have those students four mornings a week. She also suggested adding a fifth day. And that's what they did. The principal later called her into his office and asked her what else they should do with the program, and she said they should add three-year-olds. They did that as well. For every decision about the program, the administration asked Andra's expert advice, which she gladly gave.

Andra was devastated when they started interviewing candidates for the three-year-old preschool. It was her idea to add that age group. It was her idea to add another day to the program. Now that they were going to hire another teacher, Andra was no longer working full-time. She was no longer able to earn a living wage, though this program had been her idea in the first place.

What would you like to tell your principal (if there were no consequences)?

I believe that by having 4-year-olds in school only a half day, we are compromising our education system. We should expand it to a full day. Kids would get more out of it, and it would be good for parents too.

What would you like to hear your principal finally say?

What do you want? Let's make that happen!

What else would you like to say?

It upsets me because I feel like most administrators have taught older children. They don't understand what happens and why it happens in preschool. If I call my principal into my room to see something really cool that we're doing, he says, "Oh that's great! They seem so happy." Well yes, they are happy, but that's not the point. The point is how they are learning and experiencing the world. Most administrators only seem to care that the kids are safe and happy. They don't show any interest as to why the learning activities are important.

One day the principal came in when the kids were putting building blocks around other kids' bodies as they were lying on the floor. She never asked what the kids were getting out of it. I love it when my mom comes in to help me in class because, after forty-five years of experience, she really gets it! She will come up to me and tell me about a kid getting something after struggling with it all year, and we will celebrate that.

Lauren H.

Age 34

10 years
Art/English teacher

Lauren has big, brown eyes and an easy smile. As an art teacher, her outfits are often creative, colorful, and coordinated. She is sleek and hip. She loves being with kids and is very well liked.

In junior college Lauren was taking tons of art classes, as well as child development classes. Her child development teacher was enthusiastic and well-educated. Her passion was infectious, and she inspired Lauren to want to teach.

Lauren loves making connections with students. Forming community is more important than any curriculum could be. She hates apathy: students' lack of motivation results in destructive behavior and affects everyone.

A principal really came through for Lauren doing her first year at her current school. She was having a difficult time with a particular 6th grade group. They were awful to her. Lauren would give out gag prizes in her classroom just for fun. One day she gave out some packets of Taco Bell hot sauce as a joke. This group of students asked if they could drink it in class, and she said that they could.

All the students agreed to tell their parents that Lauren had forced them to drink a packet of hot sauce if they wanted an A. Lauren was subsequently called into the principal's office. The principal told Lauren that some angry parents had called, but not to worry. She wanted to hear Lauren's side of the story before the meeting continued. Lauren explained that she was giving out the hot sauce as a gag prize, and that the students had lied about her saying they had to drink it if they wanted an A. The principal completely understood and didn't blame Lauren at all. The way the situation was handled was caring and thoughtful. The principal really cushioned the harshness of that experience for her, and Lauren will be forever grateful.

Lauren hasn't had many experiences where a principal has let her down, but there have been a few. She had been teaching preschool in Humboldt and was getting along great with the lead teacher. One day, the school paid for the employees to go out to lunch together, to get to know each other better. Lauren had mentioned her "partner," and the lead teacher asked a question about "him." Lauren replied with the word "she," and the lead teacher's demeanor immediately changed. Realizing that Lauren was in a same-sex relationship made the lead teacher stiffen up and completely change the way she acted toward her.

Later that year, Lauren received a terrible performance review. She brought it to the attention of the Head Start supervisor and said that she didn't understand why she had gotten a bad evaluation. Her first evaluation had been glowing, and her performance at the job hadn't changed. Lauren didn't mention that she felt as if her coming out to the head teacher was the reason for the bad performance review. Instead of agreeing to come in and observe Lauren herself, which is what Lauren was hoping for, the Head Start District Supervisor said, "Well, why don't we wait and see how the next review looks and take it from there?"

Lauren ended up getting sick with mono and was unable to go back to work for a while. Eventually she just quit. Lauren felt discriminated against for who she was. The supervisors acted irresponsibly because her review did not reflect her performance. Homophobia and bigotry were obviously the causes of her bad evaluation.

What would you like to tell your principal (if there were no consequences)?

We are grossly underpaid. Why is there such a huge pay differential between the teacher's salary and the principal's? We do way more work. The funds should be more evenly distributed. There is no reason a principal should make $120,000/year, when a teacher barely makes $40,000. After ten years, I'm barely making 50,000.

What would you like to hear your principal finally say (or do)?

I want them to teach one class per day while they are the principal. That way they can NEVER forget what it's like to be a teacher and deal with kids all day. It's easy to sit back and tell teachers what classes should be like, but it's another thing to be in the midst of it and understand how challenging it can really be.

Karen

Age 46

17 years
Grades 7-8 English, History, Social Studies

Karen is stylish and pretty, yet she has an "in-charge" demeanor. You can tell that she loves her students and is well loved in return.

Karen became a teacher because she had some inspiring teachers when she was in school. The most inspiring was her sixth-grade teacher, Mrs. Perkins. Karen loves teaching middle school because at that age they still care. They have a desire to please you and are eager to learn. The thing she hates most about teaching is all the grading and the paperwork. Her school gets out at 2:30 pm, but the day I interviewed her she didn't leave school until 4:30. And she still had a couple more hours of work to finish up before tomorrow.

Karen's worst moment as a teacher was when a student told her that she was being sexually abused by her uncle. Karen had to get the authorities involved, and she almost had to go to court. That was heart-breaking and overwhelming.

Her best moments are watching kids grow up and being invited to their weddings and baby showers. This is something that has happened frequently.

Karen recently made the national news. She had done an activity in her middle school English classes that she had learned about on the internet. She had the students write down something they were worried about. Then all the "worries" were crumpled into a ball and thrown toward the front of the room. They were read out loud one-by-one. The atmosphere in the room was serene, quiet, and respectful. Everyone started to realize (including Karen), what kinds of things each child was going through. Some of them were worried about their parents' divorce, and others were worried about who to sit with; they felt they had no friends. After the worries were read, they were placed in a plastic bag and hung by the door. The message was: "These are your stories. You can honor and acknowledge them, but you don't need to carry them around with you. Leave them at the door. They are a part of you, but they are not who you are."

A local Oklahoma news channel interviewed a few students who expressed how important this experience was to them and how much this teacher (Karen) had changed their lives. The video clip went viral the day before I interviewed Karen. The principal was great about allowing some coverage, but also maintaining some boundaries. She could not have handled it better. Karen wants to thank her principal for this support because none of this was planned.

One of the worst times Karen had with a principal was during her second year; he told her "Don't ever hug kids." Karen was not ok with this mandate. She told him, "If a kid needs a hug, I will give it to them, and nothing you say can stop me. In some cases this is the only hug a student will ever get, and they need to know they are cared about and loved."

Karen once had a principal that had been a teacher and then got promoted to principal. He had been the principal for less than a month, when he started acting all "holier than thou." He was on a power trip and treated his former colleagues (teachers) as "just lowly teachers."

What would you like to tell your principal (if there were no consequences)?

Why can't we wear jeans at school and still look professional? It would make me happy to wear jeans, be comfortable, and not have to be in pants every day.

What would you like to hear your principal finally say?

Absolutely you can wear jeans. It doesn't affect your teaching ability, so you can if you want to.

What else would you like to say?

I would like more collaboration, fellowship, team building, and Christmas parties. Some schools are good at this, but my current school isn't. People don't really socialize together.

Lauren J.

Age 28

5 years
Grade 2

Lauren is a slim woman with youthful, light energy. She smiles often and is thoughtful about everything she does. She is passionate about learning and human development.

Lauren originally wanted to be a nurse. In college she realized she didn't do well with blood and guts, so it quickly became apparent that nursing wasn't for her. She was really enjoying her childhood development class, though. Lauren realized she could be a teacher. She developed a fascination with brain development and how kids learn.

The thing Lauren loves most about teaching is when a student is struggling with something, and suddenly they "get it." It lights up their whole face and ignites their excitement for learning. This is called the "light-bulb" moment for good reason.

Lauren hates the pressure from society to be a cookie-cutter, straight-edge type of person. The person that comes to her mind is "Miss Honey" from the Matilda movie. She is always happy and nice. People want you to not drink or go out after 8:00 pm; these are things that Lauren sometimes enjoys doing.

Her best moment occurred with a student named David who could not read at all. He was many levels behind at the beginning of the year and couldn't even put sounds together. By the end of the year, not only had he learned to read, but he loved to read. Lauren considers this one of her greatest successes.

Lauren's worst moment occurred during her first year of teaching. Her classroom management was so bad that she was given a lecture saying that if it didn't improve, she would be let go. She felt like she was sinking. Lauren thinks this is not something that can really be taught in educator preparation classes. Fortunately, the school offered her a great mentor, a retired teacher named Barbara who would come into her classroom and write notes about what Lauren could do better. After Barbara left each day, Lauren would read the notes and implement those changes. Her classroom management improved dramatically.

Lauren's principal had her back during a Student Support Team meeting. The parents started to be hostile toward Lauren, blaming her for the way things were going for their child. Immediately her principal spoke up. She had frequently been in Lauren's classroom, and none of what they had accused her of had actually happened. The principal completely shut those parents down, and they didn't speak disrespectfully to Lauren from that moment on.

Lauren can't remember any specific times when she has been let down by her administrator. Generally, she has felt supported. There are things she would like more of, however, such as positive feedback. Teachers are asked to do more and more, and they are continually criticized the whole time for doing things wrong. It's hard to know when they are doing a good job; Lauren would like to hear that from time to time.

**What would you like to tell your principal
(if there were no consequences)?**

It's nice to be acknowledged for a job well done. We are getting more and more put on us, including more criticism. There is no positive feedback.

What would you like to hear your principal finally say?

I walked in and observed the students all learning. You're doing a great job.

What else would you like to say?

There are a lot of ups and downs in teaching. This interview could have gone very differently if it had been at the end of a long day, and I wasn't feeling so positive. You feel like everything you do is never enough. But to see the outcome of learning is a great feeling. This is why I do it.

Justus

Age 33

4 years
Middle/High School Math and PE

Justus is an outgoing and energized teacher. He has a beard and glasses. He used to be known for his long hair, but it is now short. He loves to joke with students, and he is passionate about math. You can tell from being around him that Justus loves almost everything about teaching. He is truly in his element at school.

Justus tried to run away from teaching but was unsuccessful. His mother was a teacher, his aunts were teachers, and his grandmother was a teacher. Justus got a math degree in college and planned to use it for some sort of engineering work. He then moved out to California because of a girl. During that time, he started substitute teaching at a charter school, and found that he had a knack for it. Classroom management came very easily to him, and he loved the attention his comedic rants received; the students were a captive audience. His relationship didn't work out; they broke up early in the school year. However, Justus was enjoying his job, so he decided to stay in California, at least until the end of the school year. Then he decided to become a full-time teacher; he figured it couldn't be more difficult than substituting. When his current job came open, he interviewed on a Thursday and started teaching the following Monday. Everything just fell into place.

Justus loves interacting with the students more than anything. He also loves disseminating information. He hates that he feels like he is trying to sell a product to a consumer who doesn't want or need it. He hates the question: When am I ever going to use this? The truth is he doesn't know. They might never have to use it. Students are not intrinsically motivated to learn math. It doesn't help that they receive negative messages from home about math.

Justus has found himself in a bar from time to time, telling a stranger that he is a math teacher. The person will immediately say, "Oh I hated math." Why is this ok? You would never meet someone in a bar, tell them you are an English teacher, and have the person cheerfully respond, "Oh, I am illiterate!" It's so frustrating.

His best moments are when he comes up with the perfect metaphor to explain something, or a kid finally gets something after struggling with it. He loves seeing them succeed.

His worst moment as a teacher comes every November. Students don't seem to be getting it, and he feels like he's not doing anything right. The end of the year is still very far away. It's just a hard month to get through.

Justus has always felt supported by his current principal, Deborah. With the increasing use of technology, she makes sure he has all the equipment he needs to do his job.

The principal before Deborah didn't seem to do much of anything. If he sent a student out, the student would return to the class very quickly. She didn't see a problem with the behavior at all.

**What would you like to tell your principal
(if there were no consequences)?**

Make sure you realize you are the head of the organization. Your choices will dictate how the school runs. Don't get bogged down in the day-to-day details. Support your teachers. Be a resource.

What would you like to hear your principal finally say?

Encouraging words are always great, but don't do it like they do in elementary school. They say "Oh you're doing such a great job on that," and you know it's just horseshit. It should be real, genuine praise.

Logan

Age 37

Logan is a tall man; he stands at least a head above everyone in the school. He has a sleepy demeanor and a wry, sarcastic sense of humor. While his demeanor seems negative at first, he can elicit laughter with every comment he makes.

Logan became a teacher because he had a "pretty cruddy" childhood. His mother left when he was 9, and while she was there, she wasn't great anyway. He grew up in poverty, surrounded by drugs. People around him were in and out of prison, and he grew up in trailer parks. However, Logan always loved his teachers; they were there for him in ways that his parents were not. He has always loved academia, specifically higher order thinking.

Logan loves helping people to think and move up in the world. He loves people, ideas, and helping kids with their mission. So many kids need help and don't have the adults around to foster that growth.

He doesn't hate anything about teaching, because hate is a strong word. It's tough to teach nowadays because of generational problems; each lesson needs to be reinvented to meet new demands. Logan dislikes paperwork and grading, having politicians bash teachers, and, of course, the pay. He also doesn't like the "well you chose this job so don't complain about the money" attitude that people have toward teachers.

Logan never stops thinking about teaching, ever. He is always thinking about what to do in class, ways to scaffold lessons for kids. Even in his sleep, he has nightmares about teaching. He thinks, and even dreams, about teaching all summer long. One of Logan's Best moments was when he was working at a court school. Kids were sent there after they were kicked out of regular school. This school had been chewing through teachers at an alarming rate. Logan was able to get some control of the kids, and he helped improve the campus. It was tough making such serious decisions about kids' lives. Logan knew that if he recommended it, they would be sent to juvenile hall. This decision would affect the rest of their lives. He had to send some kids there, but it was a tough call to make.

Another rewarding moment in his teaching career was when Logan was the debate coach. He never expected this, but his team competed at the state level and actually won a medal.

Some of the worst moments for Logan are when parents rip into him. He had a kid once who was pulling the keys of the chrome book with a butter knife, and the parents would not do anything about it. He had a counselor come into his classroom and yell at him in front of his class, because a student he had sent out had a hard home life, and the counselor thought Logan wasn't "considering that." He has had students call him names and tell the principal he was a "piece of shit," and that was just casually written into the administrator's notes. He gets that kids can be jerks, because they are still developing; that's understandable, but adults?

Logan's current principal has backed him up 100%. In general, she doesn't let people push her around, but she does it on the down low, so no one notices. Overall, she is one of the best. He has had many bad administrators, but only a few good ones.

During his first few years of teaching, Logan was often let down by his principals. In his first year, he had to sit through a two-hour lecture his principal gave about how teaching is like a basketball game. That was disappointing. Not everyone can relate to basketball.

What would you like to tell your principal (if there were no consequences)?

The further removed you get from the classroom, the harder it is to get an idea of what's happening in class. Everything is different now; it's always changing. Even since 2016, the speed of the game is a lot more intense. Lessons need to be much more flexible now.

What would you like to hear your principal finally say?

We now have a full-time civics class. Not government; civics.

What else would you like to say?

Overall, Deborah has helped me out a lot.

June

Age 50

June is a short woman with wavy gray hair that changes color according to her experiments. She has glasses and youthful, light energy. She has studied brain development, teaching, and learning. She speaks and writes Spanish almost flawlessly, even though it's not her first language.

June did not choose teaching. Teaching chose her. She never wanted to be a teacher, but I always thought that she would. June is good at explaining things. She has a knack for getting people to understand even very confusing things. The teachers that she had did not.

June did not go into teaching because she "cares about children," although she does generally care about fellow humans of all ages. She didn't go into it because she felt a calling or wanted to be a leader. She always considered herself far too shy to be called a leader. She literally was looking for jobs after college and came home one afternoon to an answering machine full of messages. Someone had told someone else who told someone else that June spoke Spanish fluently, and a high school up north needed a Spanish teacher

76

ASAP. June needed a job and the school needed a teacher; it was a match.

June loves it when class goes smoothly. She values the relationship with each kid, and really being there for them, listening to them, and acknowledging them for who they are. She loves when students learn to speak Spanish fluently and voluntarily make Spanish a part of their daily life. She also loves doing fun projects with kids.

She hates that teaching can feel so overwhelming, even abusive. A police officer can call for backup if they need help, but a teacher who asks for help or "backup" is seen as weak. Other teachers will ostracize a teacher who struggles with classroom management, instead of supporting or trying to assist them. June disagrees with this "macho" attitude; she believes that everyone struggles with things at one point or another, and we should back each other up.

June's best moments as a teacher are when lessons go well and kids are really learning. She loves it when kids say they love Spanish, and she always tries to make class engaging for her students. She also has had many great times with her coworkers, lots of laughs and lasting friendships.

Her worst moments result from anxiety and the pressure she feels from others—students, administrators, other teachers, parents, the entire community—to be perfect; it's overwhelming. June is considering other careers that don't take so much out of her, yet are more rewarding both financially and emotionally.

Administrators have come through for June on many occasions. After an observation in an eighth grade Spanish class, her principal, Ms. Atkins said these exact words to her: "You know how sometimes you wonder if you should be a teacher, if you're cut out for it? Never. Ever. Say. That. Again. In all my years in schools, I have never, ever seen anything like what I saw in your classroom. Kids were engaged and really learning, and the entire lesson was in Spanish." Those words have stayed with June. She saw then that it was her destiny to teach, even though she was questioning it during her third year of teaching. Now she is in her twenty-third.

On another occasion, June was teaching high school Spanish. She had a rather small class that usually behaved for her. She wasn't emotionally prepared when they started to misbehave, especially since she thought of them as her "good" class (big mistake by the way). One day some of the boys started acting up. June doesn't remember exactly what happened, just that she sent one of the boys out of class and the others kept laughing at her, so she lost it and sent out two more.

After class June went to speak with her principal, Mr. Rojas. He was new to the school, so she didn't know him well. In fact, she didn't know him at all. In his office, she explained that she kicked out one of the boys, then she "freaked out" and kicked out the other two. (Never before had June dismissed more than one student at a time.) She was so embarrassed about her lack of control, but she was honest about her embarrassment as well. She started crying, sure that he was going to fire her for being such a mess. Mr. Rojas just sat back in his chair and, instead of scolding or firing her, said "What else is bothering you?" She proceeded to tell him that the other member of the Spanish department, Jane, had suddenly stopped talking to June and she didn't know why. They had been such good friends before, and June was convinced that it was because the files were messy when June put them back. June apologized for crying. Mr. Rojas replied, "Listen, June, it's ok. All I have to do all day long is wait around for problems to happen. So, cry away, as much as you'd like. What else is bothering you?"

Conversely, principals have let June down on many occasions as well. Most often, they said that they would "take a walk" down to the classroom to help out, and then they end up forgetting, or just not showing up. June once had a very challenging 6th grade class on Tuesdays, right before lunch, from 11:00am to 11:45. June's principal told her that she cannot ask for help on Tuesdays because everyone was in meetings, but on any other day feel free to call for help. Overall, just being put off, treated as not important, or administrators not taking her concerns or subject matter seriously have been the major issues. Another source of discouragement is her being left out while others are continuously praised and acknowledged. After 23 years, it gets a little tiring to hear how amazing everyone is (except you).

June's biggest pet-peeve is when she tells her administrator about a bad behavior that is happening in her class/school, and they act shocked. They act as if they have no idea things like that are happening there, and ask if she is sure. In a previous school, when June told the principal that the 7th graders were banging on the lockers loudly on their way to their Spanish class, the principal gasped in confusion. She claimed she had NO IDEA anything like that was going on.

This last one has only happened once in June's teaching career: having a principal who takes the kids' side and supports their complaint that she is "mean and unfair." Really, it's the teacher who needs support, and to be thrown under the bus again and again this past year has been deeply disappointing for June.

What would you like to tell your principal (if there were no consequences)?

Do NOT believe the kids over the teachers. If students say that a teacher is mean and "a bitch" and unfair, and they did absolutely nothing except be a perfect angel, do NOT believe them. And for Christ's sake, certainly do not agree with them! Students express themselves with behavior. Do not interpret their words literally, as a fundamentalist Christian would interpret the Bible! If a student says that a teacher is mean, it means that the kids are being mean to the teacher, and the teacher is trying to handle it but not able to do so effectively. It means the kids are harassing him/her, and that teacher needs your support more than anything. Kids "speak" through their behavior. Don't always take their words literally.

What would you like to hear your principal finally say?

I know your job is hard, and I want you to know that you are handling it phenomenally. I will be here to back you up for whatever you need. You are valuable to our school. Just let me know what you need, and I'll come through for you.

Conclusion

A principal is not only a conglomeration of their tasks: evaluate teachers, discipline students, assuage parents, do paperwork. A principal cannot not look back on their day and say: "Well, I've done this and this and that, so I did a good job. Here is the paper trail to prove it." When a principal has truly completed their job for the day, the results cannot be measured on paper. The results will show in teachers who feel confident, valued, appreciated, and safe. The students will feel this way as well. I don't know if that can be measured, but I know it can be felt. The results will be clearly reflected in the students' learning, knowledge, and positive school concept. In an atmosphere that is respectful, kids will learn to respect and be respected. That's why a principal's job is critical.

Take teachers seriously. Don't look the other way when the kids are disrespectful. Actually care how they are feeling. Actually do something. Act like you care about the teachers. Reflect upon how it might feel to be a teacher in your school. How can you make it a better experience? Tell teachers that you have their back, no matter what, and then demonstrate that. Your job is not only in service of the students and their parents. You are the protector of the teachers. You are the keeper of our dignity. No matter who we are, we matter, and we are your charge. Each teacher has their strengths and weaknesses, but we are all committed to doing the best possible job we can. When you minimize our concerns or tell us you're too busy to help us, it's more than inconvenient. On an emotional plane, you're telling us we don't matter. It's sort of like punching us in the stomach. It is scary to be honest about any problems we are having because most of us rely on our salary for basic survival. It doesn't feel safe to admit we are struggling, and the truth is that everyone struggles. That's because we are all human. You should say things that will make us not be afraid. Increase our courage. Increase our joy. You are like a parent… so bring surprise goodies, if you are able to. Thank us for our sacrifices. Wonder how we are feeling. Ask us. Try to fix it if we're down or needing help.

We do not feel indifferent toward our principals. We love them or we hate them. Being the defender of our dignity is a huge job. The most important thing is to always act with kindness and empathy. Teachers' feelings and thoughts are invisible, but they are real.

Of course teaching is about the kids. We want to educate them academically, emotionally, and socially. We want to meet their needs, as they are human beings who are developing. However, teachers are people too. While we are focusing on the kids' needs, and the administrative scheduling needs, often the teachers' needs get bulldozed. It's time to start treating teachers as human beings as well. Teachers are more likely than our students to not have our needs met. We need to feel respected and safe, to use the bathroom, to eat a snack. We need to connect with others, to laugh, to feel friendship. We need to lower our stress levels so we can access our own thoughts and plan the best lessons possible. We need to feel that someone has our back no matter how difficult a situation may be.

Some of us love examining data. Some of us hate it. Some of us want more feedback and support. Some of us want to be left alone. We all want to be trusted. We all want to be valued. We all need to be acknowledged for what we do. Teaching is not like any other job on the planet. It requires a great deal of collaboration on a personal and professional level. It requires friendship and trust. It requires that administrators have the wisdom to use their power in a way that helps, never harms.

What do we want to say to our administrators?

You should get to know teachers on a personal level and make more of an effort to do so at the beginning of the year. You should be interested in us, our strengths, and what we would want to work on this year.

I don't want to lose you....I would not be able to work with someone who told me what to do and tried to control the details of my job.

The opinions that other staff might have of me shouldn't be used against me. New teachers should have the support they need. It should NOT be a once-a-week check-in.... Start with the positive feedback just like we do in IEP meetings. This makes people feel good, and new teachers could use some of that. They should really monitor how that person is doing.

I know when I have class and I have a planning period, but there are things I'm not able to get done because I keep getting interrupted. When am I supposed to do those things? Also, I want you to make sure I am taking my lunch. Half the time I couldn't take it because I was so busy catching up or helping students. As the behavior specialist, behaviors happen all day long, they don't stop because it's my lunch time.

I am an intelligent, valued professional who can make decisions that are best for kids. I have three degrees, and they don't give you three degrees if you are an idiot. You should acknowledge the enormous workload we have and listen and value teachers' decisions and opinions.

I want you to teach one class per day while you are the principal. That way you can NEVER forget what it's like to be a teacher and deal with kids all day. It's easy to sit back and tell teachers what classes should be like, but it's another thing to be in the midst of it and understand how challenging it really can be.

I've been very lucky with the principals that I've had. I belong to Facebook groups of teachers and I've heard horror stories. I want you to know that the principal makes an enormous difference in the school.

You should realize that every teacher makes hundreds, sometimes thousands, of decisions every day. We are human. We always have the students' best interest at heart, but we will make mistakes from time to time.

Treat others the way you want to be treated. Don't be nasty to teachers.

Status and appearance aren't everything. We are here for the students.... It's time to stop only caring about money. Low performing schools and overcrowded classes are only profitable for people at the top. You need to switch the focus back onto the kids.

Just relax. Let teachers do what they do and trust that they are the experts…. We are okay, just trust us. You don't need to be in charge of so much. Enjoy this more. Relax.

Stop giving us so many pointless directives and guidelines; just support and trust us. We know what to do. We are professionals.

We are grossly underpaid. Why is there such a huge pay differential between the teacher's salary and the principal's? We do a lot more work. The funds should be more evenly distributed.

It's nice to be acknowledged for a job well done. We are getting more and more put on us, including more criticism. There is no positive feedback.

Make sure you realize you are the head of the organization. Your choices will dictate how the school runs. Don't get bogged down in the day-to-day details. Support your teachers. Be a resource.

Do NOT believe the kids over the teachers. If students say that a teacher is mean and "a bitch" and unfair and they did absolutely nothing except be a perfect angel, do NOT believe them. And for Christ's sakes, certainly do not agree with them! If a student says that a teacher is mean, it means that the kids are being mean to the teacher, and the teacher is trying to handle it but not able to do so effectively. It means the kids are harassing him/her, and that teacher needs your support more than anything. Kids "speak" through their behavior. Don't always take their words literally.

We should have more collaboration, fellowship, team building, and Christmas parties.

I'm worth more than you ever thought.

My goal in the classroom is to help my students listen in order to understand. If that were the main goal of administration, it would be a game-changer…. Everything would fall into place.

I'd just like to say thank you for having my back.

I'd just like to say I appreciate all that you do for me and all your kindness to me on a personal level. It means a lot.

What would we like to hear from our administrators?

Well, you say a lot of nice things. In my experience you talk the talk, but there is no follow-through. For me it's more about saying something and meaning it. And it's about honesty. I had a principal who had as an email signature that said something about not judging because you never know how much someone is struggling. This same person never lent me a helping hand when I was struggling.

When you do evaluations, why can't you talk normally? You feel the need to use "edu-babble." Why can't you admit in the start of the evaluation meeting how unfair the meetings are?

This is just busywork.

Let's recognize Carla for all the hard work she's done this week. She took care of seventy referrals! Let all acknowledge and thank Carla with a round of applause.

I'd like them to recognize that this job is hard and acknowledge me in front of others.

I'd like to hear some acknowledgement of my specific strengths in the classroom. I'd like for you to know what I was doing in class and how I was doing it.

I would like for you to come into my room and observe more often. Well, I'd like you to, but at the same time I don't want you to, because it makes me nervous. But more feedback would probably be a good thing.

I need you.

For once, I'd like to hear you publicly acknowledge that we are all of equal importance to the school.

I would like to see you be reflective on your own actions and words. There should be a 12-step program for narcissist principals to learn to treat people more kindly.

I see kids engaged in class, and all the lessons are differentiated. Good job.

Absolutely you can wear jeans. It doesn't affect your teaching ability.

We now have a full-time civics class. Not government; civics.

What do you want? Let's make that happen!

I trust you. I've got your back. I support you.

I walked in and observed the students all learning. You're doing a great job.

Encouraging words are always great, but don't do it like they do in elementary school. They say "Oh you're doing such a great job on that," and you know it's just horseshit. It should be real, genuine praise.

I know your job is hard, and I want you to know that you are handling it phenomenally. I will be here to back you up for whatever you need. You are valuable to our school. Just let me know what you need, and I'll come through for you.

I understand the situation you're in, and the challenges. I'll do anything in my power to support you.

I'm pretty sure you've said this before, but I'd like to hear: *She's doing a good job.*

If you are an administrator, you may want to ponder this: How does it feel to be a teacher in my school?

Acknowledgments

I want to sincerely thank all the participants in this book. They volunteered willingly (I did not force them to do this, although I did annoy some of them quite a bit). I only hope I did right by them in honoring their stories. I have so much gratitude and respect for these amazing teachers. May the love you give come back to you multiplied by 1000!

I also want to thank: Reyleen Jimenez, Lise Cartwright, Amy Harmanson, and Rachel Cox for putting up with me, coaching, editing and formatting, respectively. I could never have done this without you.

About the Author

Julie Bacher, M. Ed hails from Vermont, but currently resides in California. She has spent the last 23 years teaching Spanish in public schools. Bacher has also taught French, English, Cooking, Guitar, and Zentangle. She enjoys puppies, kittens, and long walks on the beach.

Self-Publishing
School

NOW IT'S YOUR TURN

Discover the EXACT 3-step blueprint you need to become a bestselling author in as little as 3 months.

Self-Publishing School helped me, and now I want them to help you with this FREE resource to begin outlining your book!

Even if you're busy, bad at writing, or don't know where to start, you CAN write a bestseller and build your best life.

With tools and experience across a variety of niches and professions, Self-Publishing School is the only resource you need to take your book to the finish line!

DON'T WAIT

Say "YES" to becoming a bestseller:

https://self-publishingschool.com/friend

Follow the steps on the page to get a FREE resource to get started on your book and unlock a discount to get started with Self-Publishing School

Can You Help?

Thank You For Reading My Book!

I really appreciate all of your feedback, and I love hearing what you have to say.

I need your input to make the next version of this book and my future books better.

Please leave me an honest review on Amazon letting me know what you thought of the book.

Thanks so much!

Julie Bacher